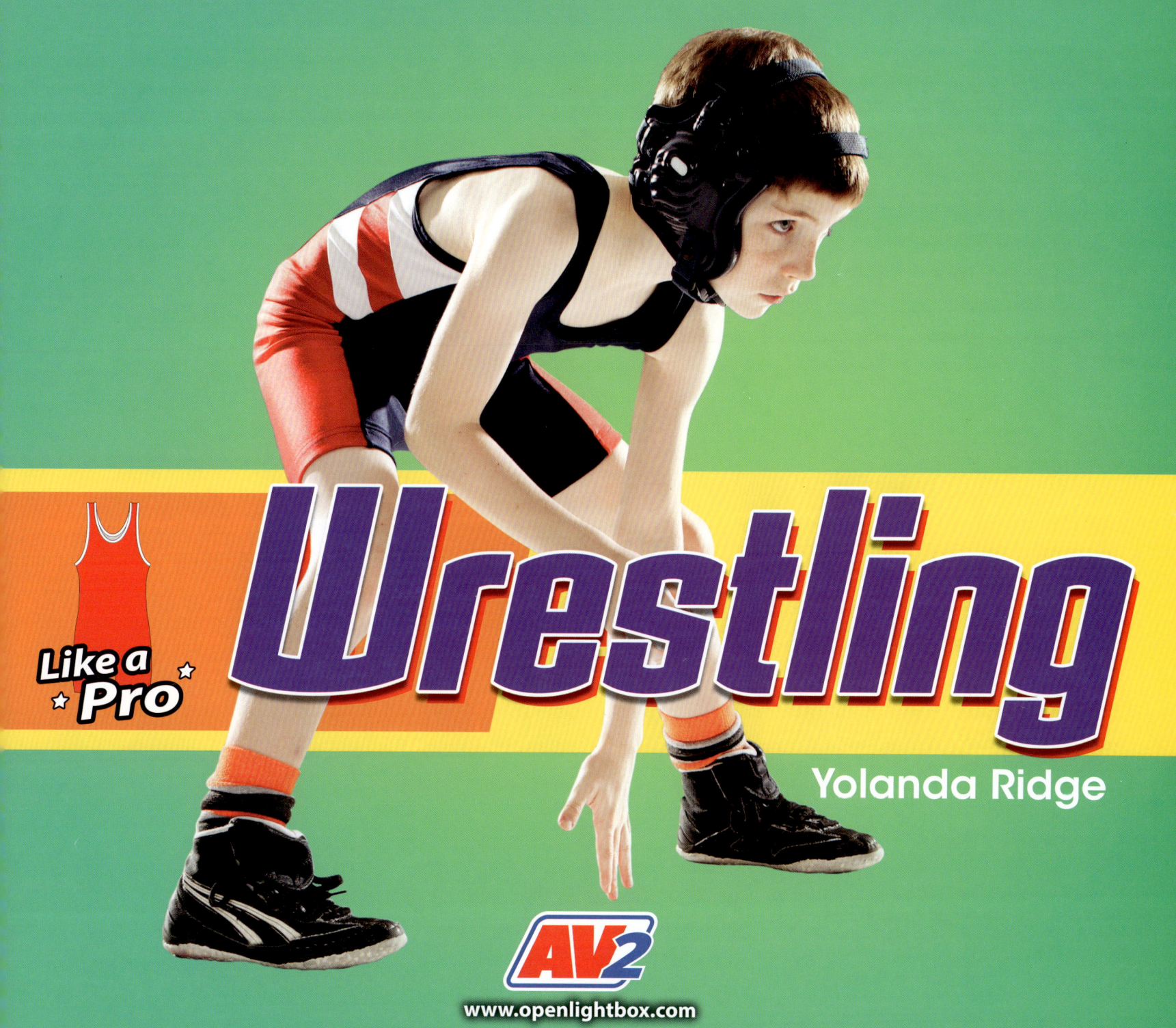

Wrestling

Like a Pro

Yolanda Ridge

Step 1
Go to **www.openlightbox.com**

Step 2
Enter this unique code
KPHSQDUPZ

Step 3
Explore your interactive eBook!

Your interactive eBook comes with...

AV2 is optimized for use on any device

|  |  |  |  |  | |  |  | |

Audio
Listen to the entire book read aloud

Videos
Watch informative video clips

Weblinks
Gain additional information for research

Try This!
Complete activities and hands-on experiments

Key Words
Study vocabulary, and complete a matching word activity

Quizzes
Test your knowledge

Slideshows
View images and captions

Share
Share titles within your Learning Management System (LMS) or Library Circulation System

Citation
Create bibliographical references following APA, CMOS, and MLA styles

This title is part of our AV2 digital subscription

1-Year K–5 Subscription
ISBN 978-1-7911-3320-7

Access hundreds of AV2 titles with our digital subscription.
Sign up for a FREE trial at **www.openlightbox.com/trial**

The digital components of this book are guaranteed to stay active for at least five years from the date of publication.

Wrestling
Like a Pro

Contents

- 2 AV2 Book Code
- 4 Getting Ready
- 6 What I Wear
- 8 What I Use
- 10 Where I Wrestle
- 12 Warming Up
- 14 Playing the Game
- 16 Winning the Game
- 18 Team Play
- 20 I Love Wrestling
- 22 Wrestling Facts
- 24 Key Words

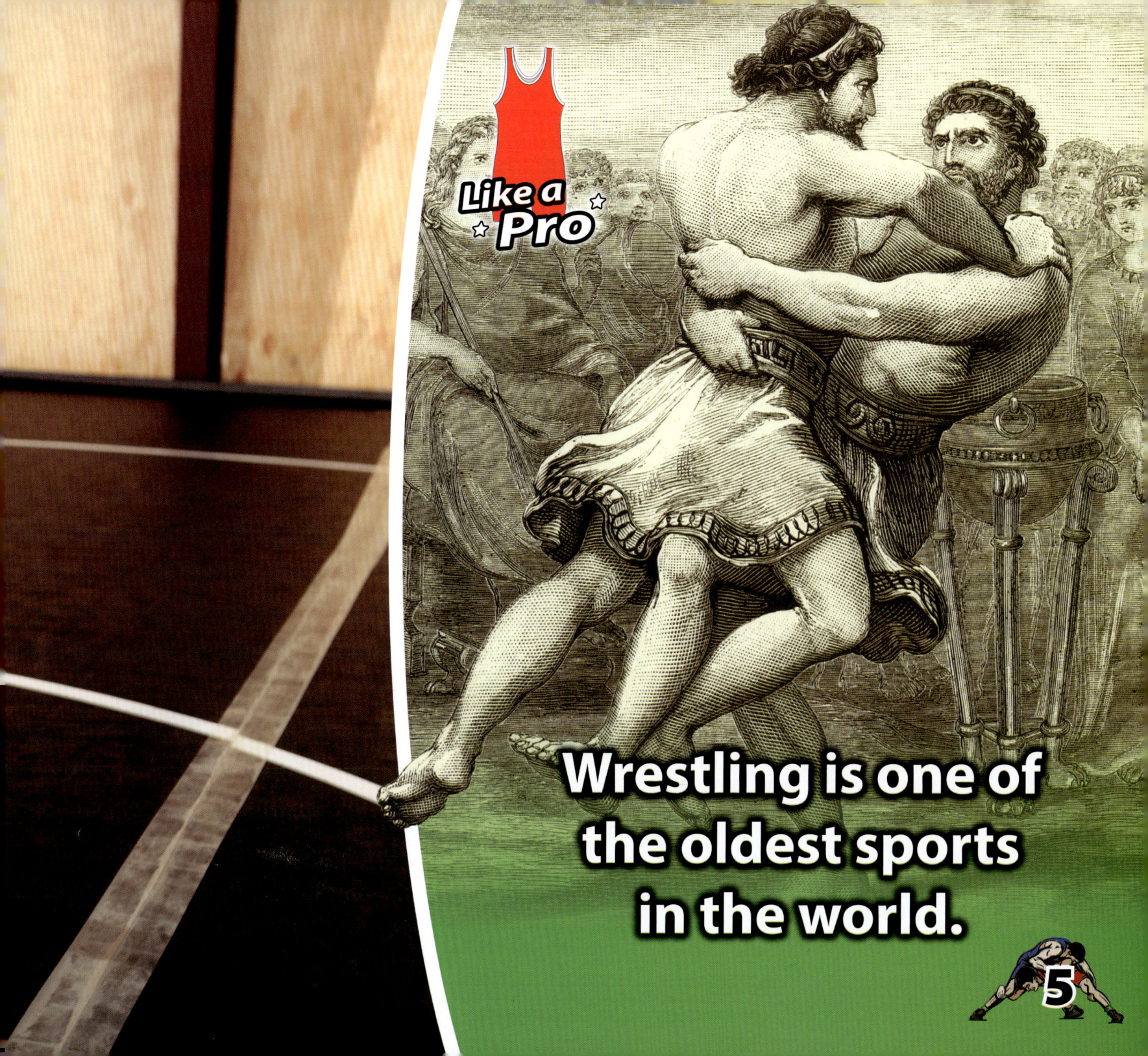

Wrestling is one of the oldest sports in the world.

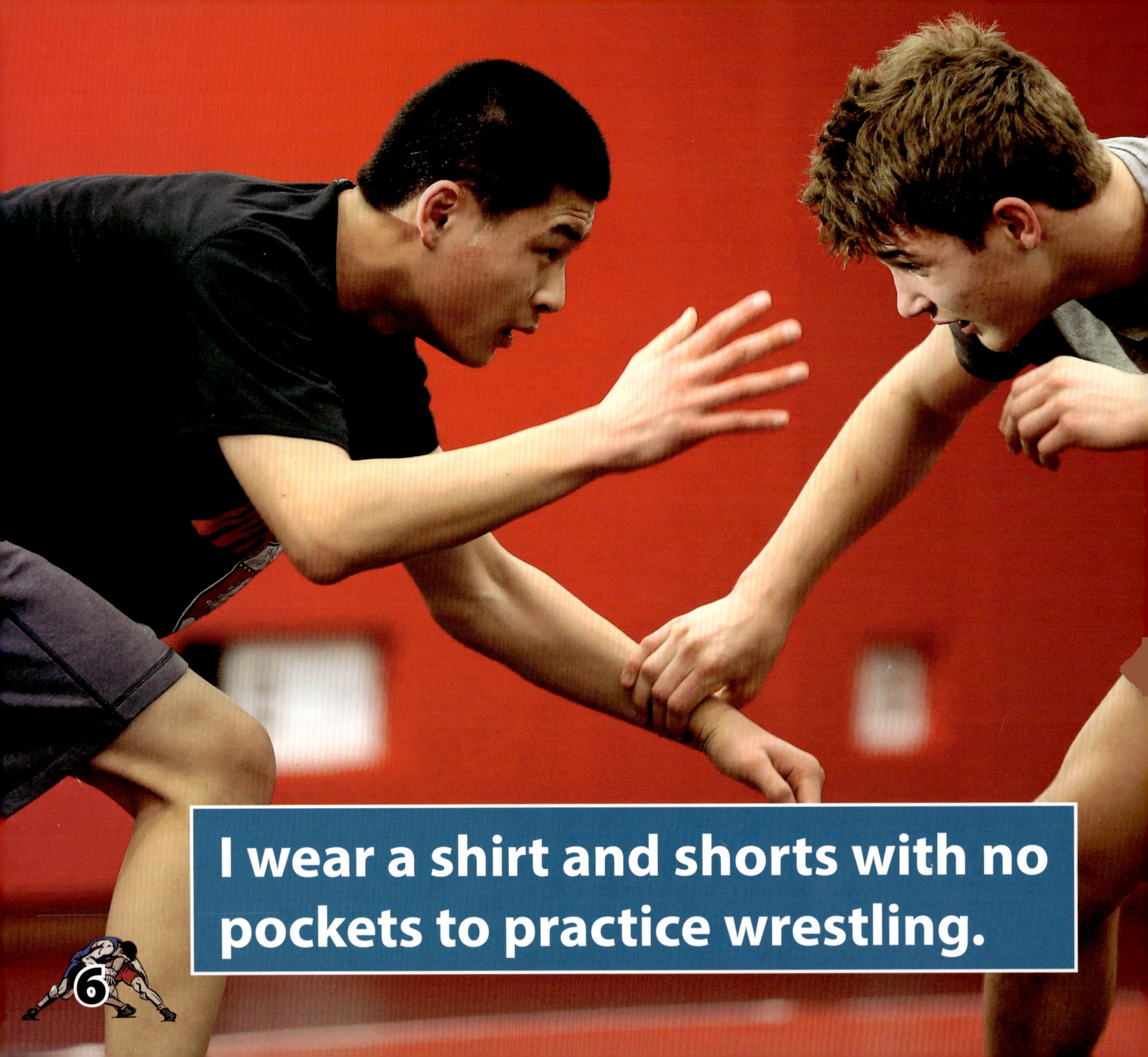
I wear a shirt and shorts with no pockets to practice wrestling.

Like a Pro

During competitions, a pro wrestler wears a piece of clothing called a singlet.

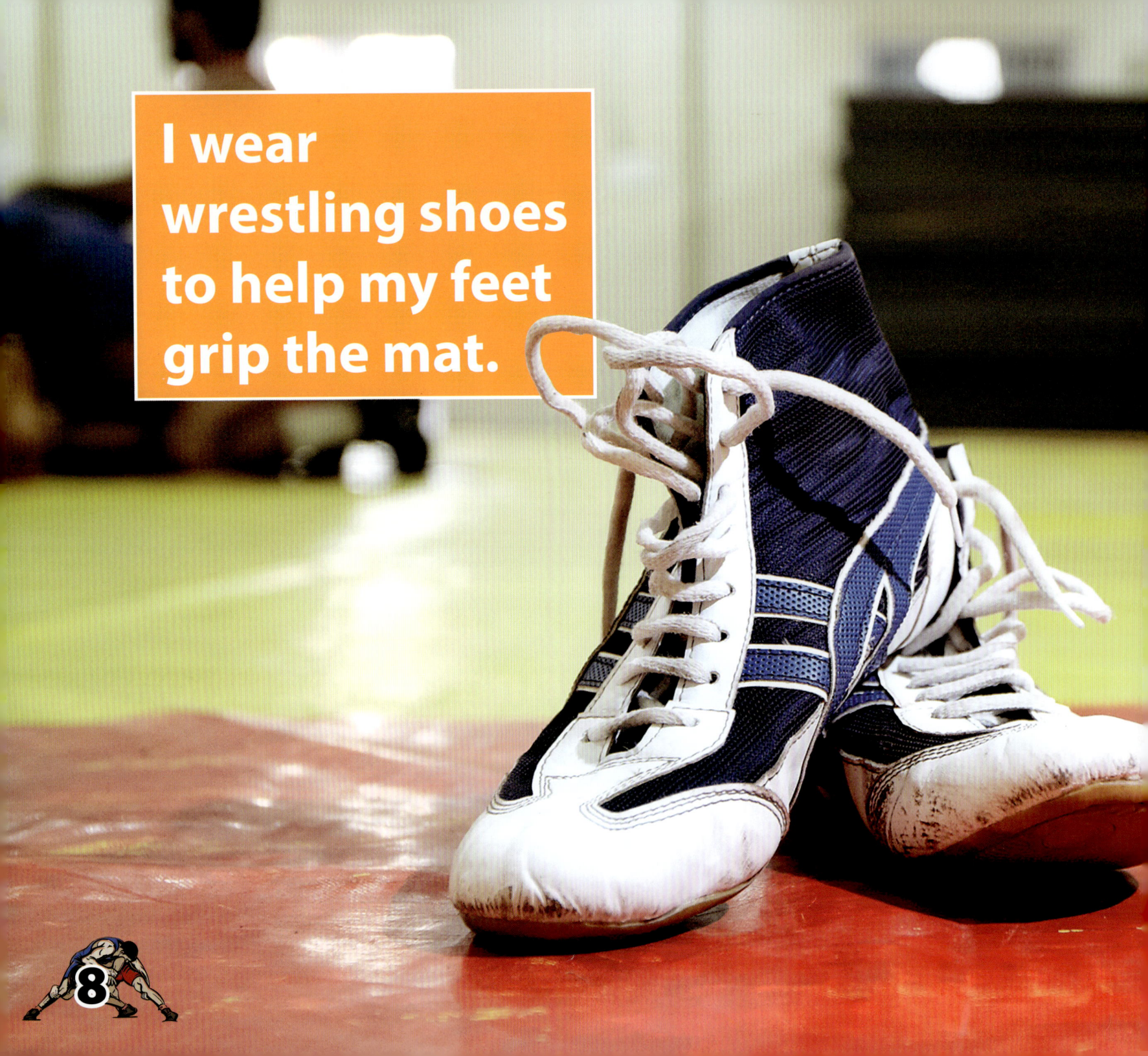

Like a Pro

Pro wrestlers may wear headgear, kneepads, and mouth guards.

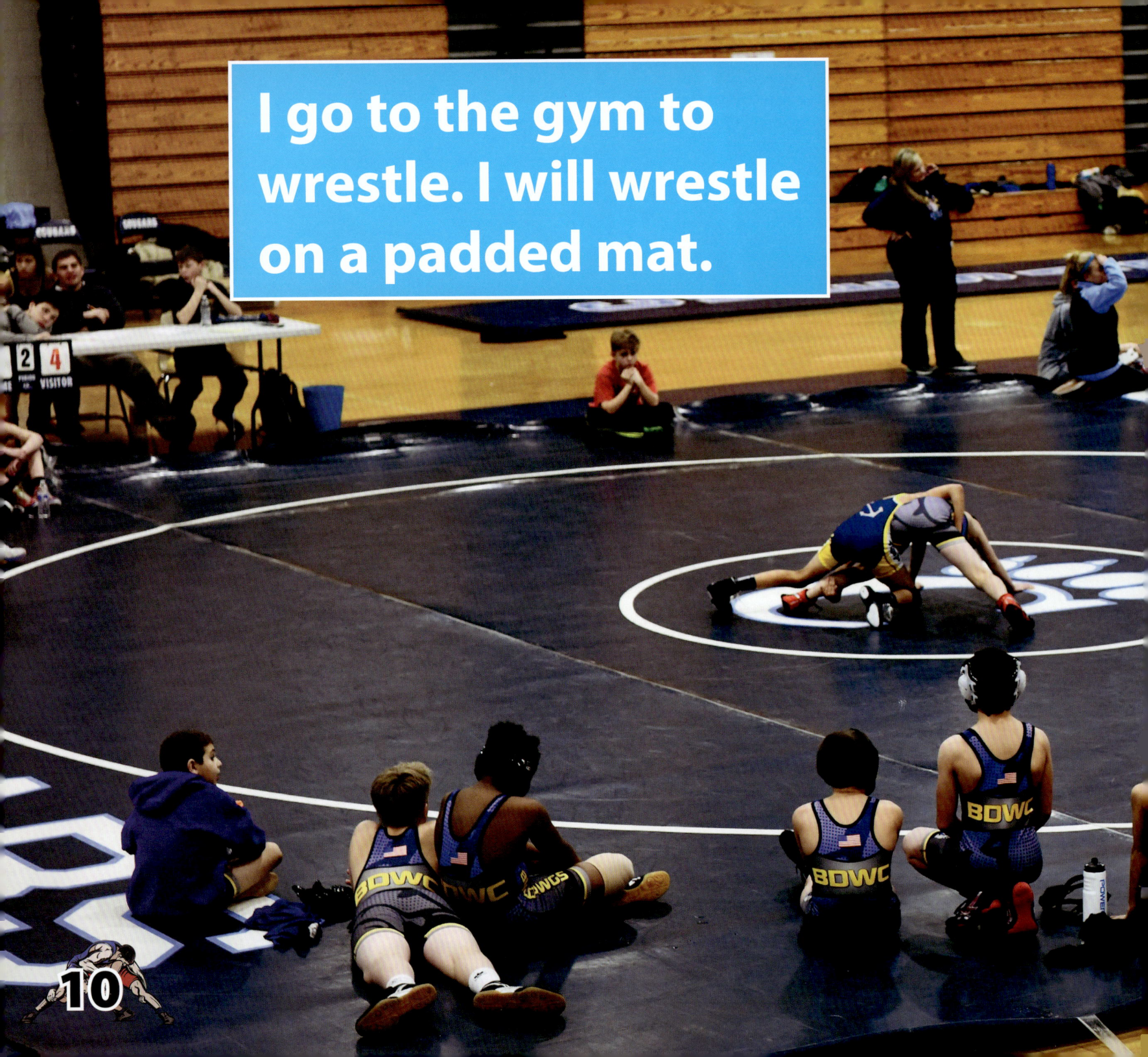

I go to the gym to wrestle. I will wrestle on a padded mat.

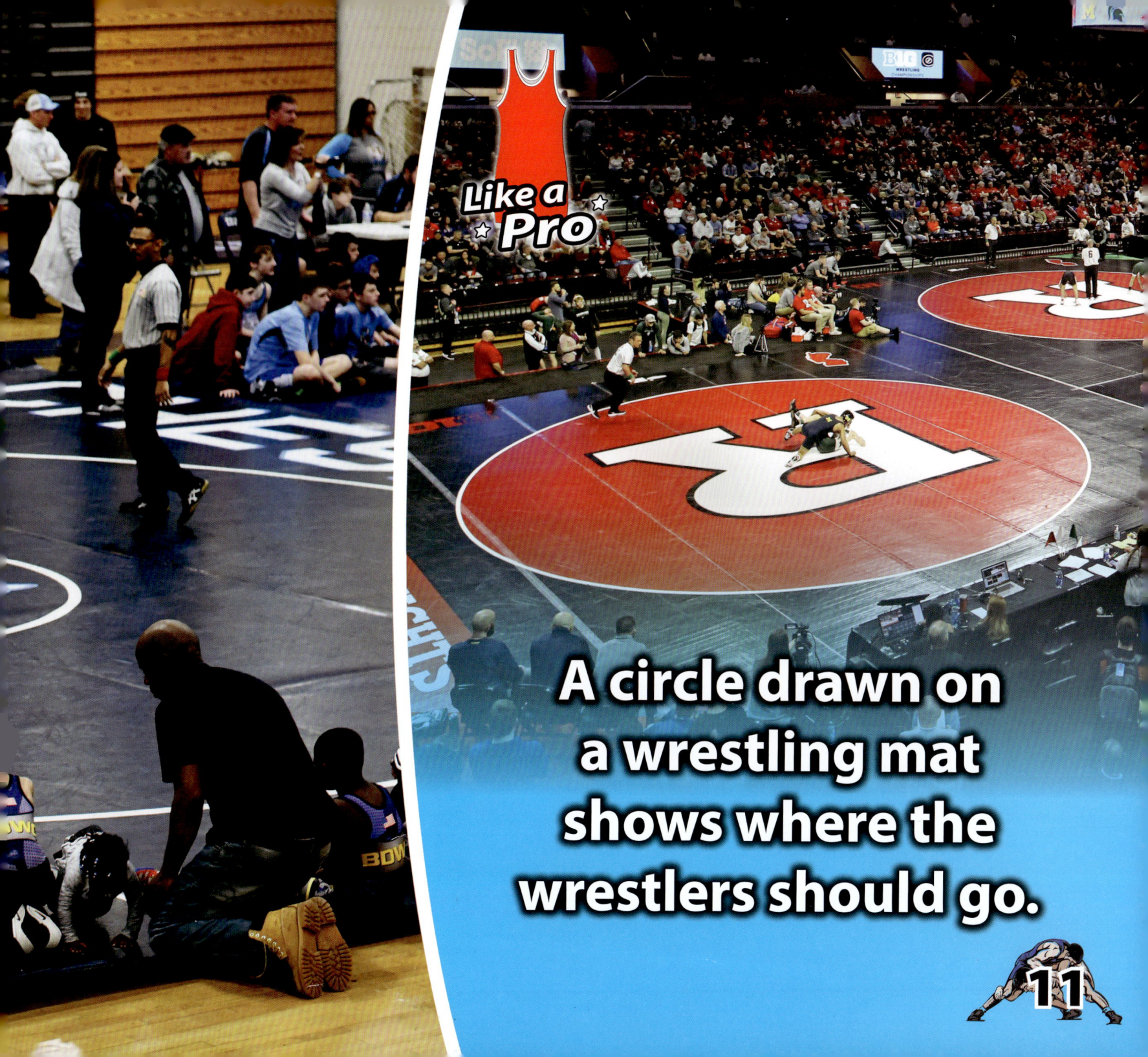

Like a Pro

A circle drawn on a wrestling mat shows where the wrestlers should go.

11

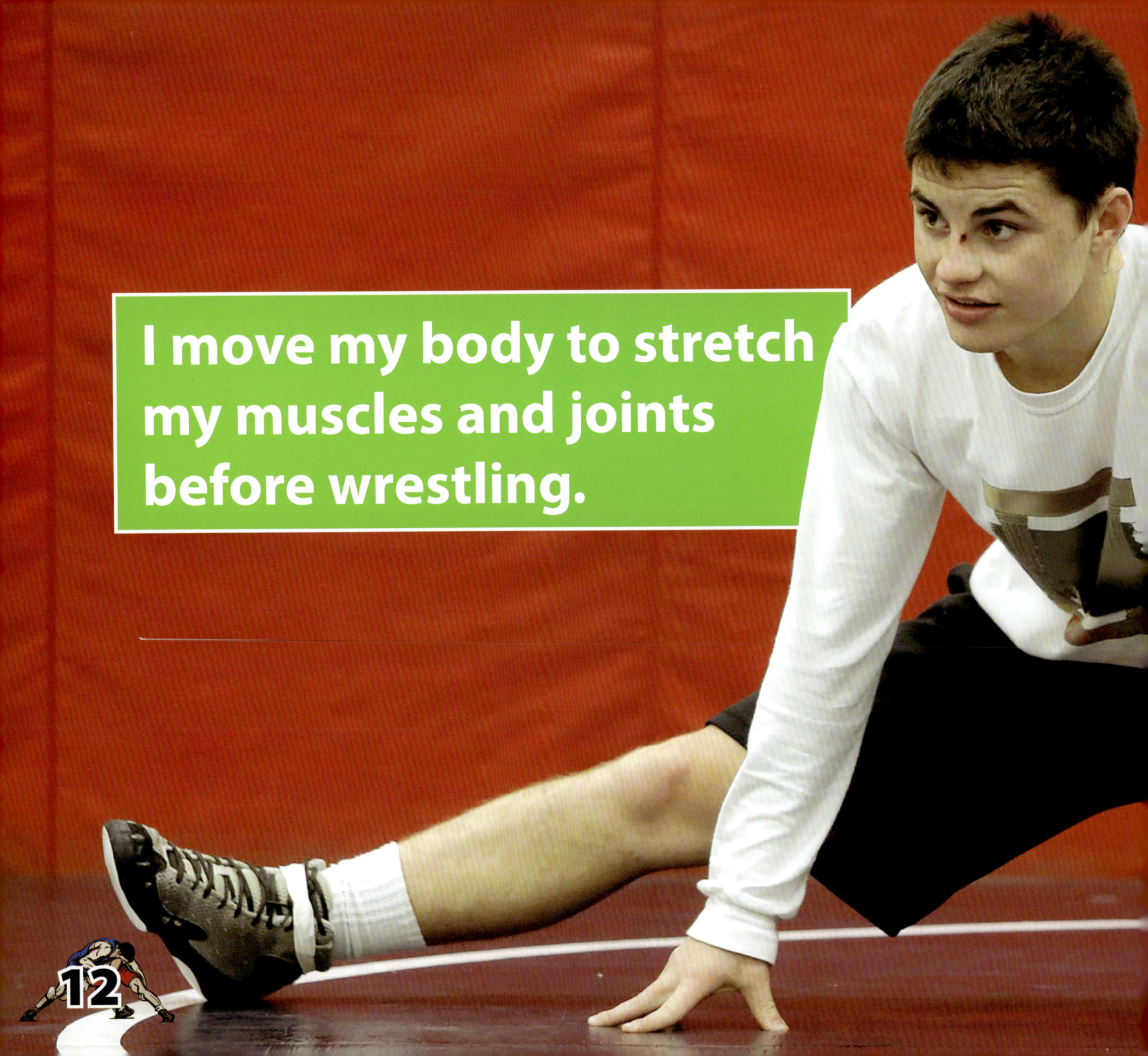

I move my body to stretch my muscles and joints before wrestling.

Like a Pro

People who are the same size wrestle against each other.

13

The other wrestler and I stand at the center of the mat. A referee blows a whistle to start the match.

There are two styles of wrestling at the Olympics.

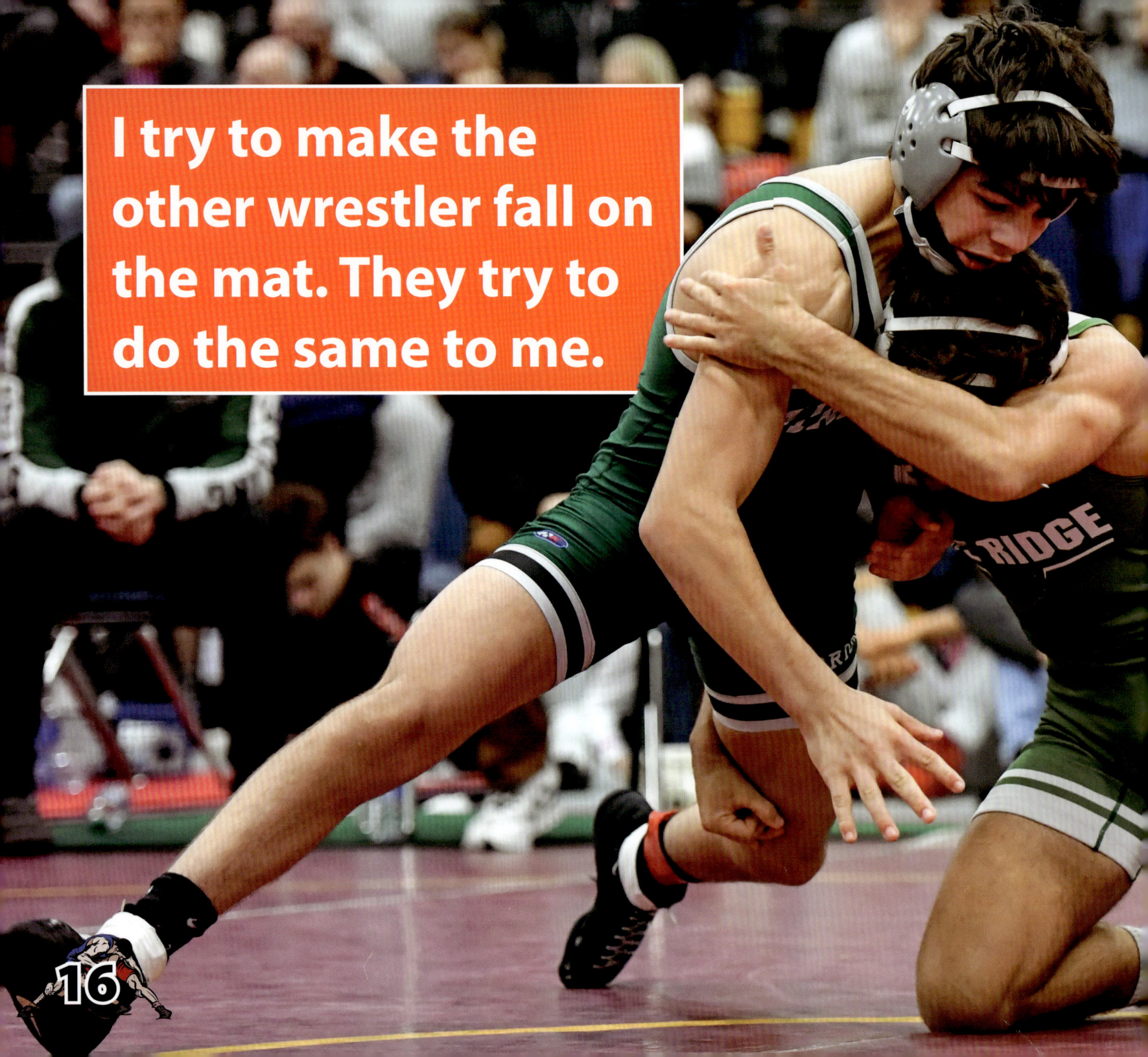

Like a Pro

If a wrestler is pinned on the mat, the other wrestler wins.

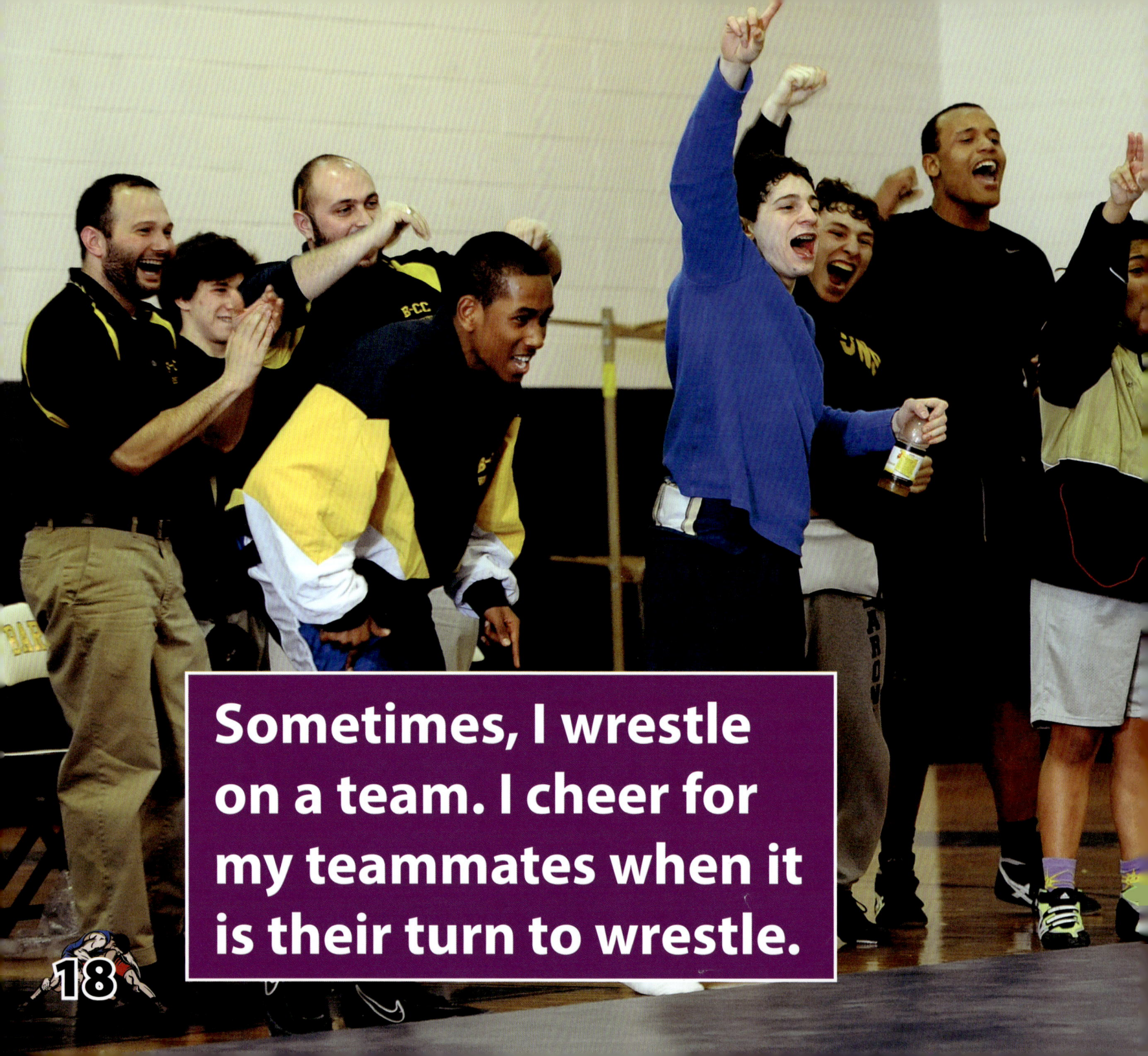

Sometimes, I wrestle on a team. I cheer for my teammates when it is their turn to wrestle.

Wrestlers earn points for certain moves. Teammates add their points together.

I love wrestling.

WRESTLING FACTS

These pages provide more detail about interesting facts found in the book. They are intended to be used by adults as a learning support to help young readers round out their knowledge of each sport featured in the *Like a Pro* series.

Pages 4–5

Getting Ready Wrestling is a sport in which two people try to get each other to lose balance. Most styles of wrestling involve a wrestler trying to hold an opponent in a certain position for some length of time. Wrestling started thousands of years ago. Cave paintings provide evidence that indicates it is one the oldest sports in the world.

Pages 6–7

What I Wear Many wrestlers will wear an athletic shirt with pocketless shorts or sweatpants, so that nothing can get caught on an opponent. A tight-fitting, one-piece uniform, called a singlet, is usually worn during competitions. At minimum, singlets cover the thighs, waist, and midsection.

Pages 8–9

What I Use Bare feet are discouraged for sanitary reasons so wrestlers must wear something on their feet. Because mats can be slippery, most wrestlers invest in wrestling shoes. Wrestling shoes are light, flexible, and grip the mat easily. Headgear, which primarily protects the ears, is often worn along with a mouth guard and kneepads to protect other areas that may strike the mat.

Pages 10–11

Where I Wrestle A standard wrestling mat has an area of 39 feet by 39 feet (12 meters by 12 meters) and is 1.2 to 2 inches (3 to 5 centimeters) thick. Depending on the type of wrestling, different lines are drawn on the mats for competition. There are usually starting lines along with circles that mark the play area.

Pages 12–13

Warming Up Dynamic stretches put muscles and joints through a full range of motion without holding them in place. This type of stretching is ideal for wrestling, as it activates certain muscles, increases flexibility, and decreases the odds of injury. Wrestlers must be in good physical condition, but can be of any size, as competitors are divided by weight class.

Pages 14–15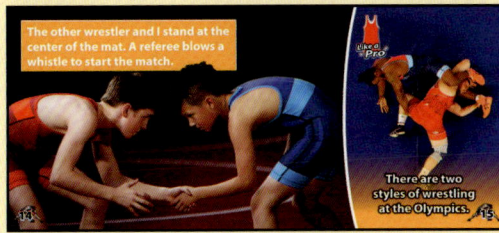

Playing the Game Wrestlers stand at the starting lines on the mat to begin a match. In both Greco-Roman and freestyle wrestling—the two styles seen in the Olympics—wrestlers use moves called holds to grab and control their opponent. In Greco-Roman wrestling, only holds above the waist are allowed. In freestyle wrestling, leg grips can be used as well.

Pages 16–17

Winning the Game In freestyle and Greco-Roman wrestling, a fall, or pin, occurs when one wrestler forces the other's shoulder blades to the mat. In international competitions, a fall is called the instant this takes place. In many school competitions, a wrestler needs to be held in position for at least a second for a fall or pin to count. A fall or pin ends the match.

Pages 18–19

Team Play If a fall or pin does not happen before the time in a match runs out, the winner is determined by points. Points are given out by a referee for successful moves, such as taking control from an opponent, or putting an opponent in danger of being pinned. In team competitions, the points awarded at the end of each match are added together to determine which team is victorious.

Pages 20–21

I Love Wrestling Many countries have their own styles of wrestling, such as sumo wrestling in Japan. International events are regulated by the Fédération Internationale de Lutte Amateur (FILA). Wrestling is valued as a sport for building confidence, athleticism, mental focus, discipline, and responsibility.

KEY WORDS

Research has shown that as much as 65 percent of all written material published in English is made up of 300 words. These 300 words cannot be taught using pictures or learned by sounding them out. They must be recognized by sight. This book contains 49 common sight words to help young readers improve their reading fluency and comprehension. This book also teaches young readers several important content words, such as proper nouns. These words are paired with pictures to aid in learning and improve understanding.

Page	Sight Words First Appearance
4	am, I
5	a, in, is, like, of, one, the, world
6	and, no, to, with
8	feet, help, my
9	may
10	go, on, will
11	should, shows, where
12	before, move
13	are, each, other, people, same, who
14	at, start
15	there, two
16	do, make, me, they, try
17	if
18	for, it, sometimes, their, turn, when
19	together

Page	Content Words First Appearance
4	wrestling
5	sports
6	pockets, shirt, shorts
7	clothing, competitions, pro wrestler, singlet
8	mat, shoes
9	headgear, kneepads, mouth guards
10	gym
11	circle
12	body, joints, muscles
13	size
14	match, referee, whistle
15	Olympics, styles
18	team, teammates
19	points

Published by Lightbox Learning Inc.
276 5th Avenue, Suite 704 #917
New York, NY 10001
Website: www.openlightbox.com

Copyright ©2024 Lightbox Learning Inc.
All rights reserved. No part of this publication may be reproduced, stored in a retrieval system, or transmitted in any form or by any means, electronic, mechanical, photocopying, recording, or otherwise, without the prior written permission of the publisher.

Library of Congress Control Number: 2023935730

ISBN 978-1-7911-5799-9 (hardcover)
ISBN 978-1-7911-5800-2 (softcover)
ISBN 978-1-7911-5801-9 (multi-user eBook)

042023
100922

Printed in Guangzhou, China
1 2 3 4 5 6 7 8 9 0 27 26 25 24 23

Project Coordinator: John Willis
Designer: Ana María Vidal

Every reasonable effort has been made to trace ownership and to obtain permission to reprint copyright material. The publisher would be pleased to have any errors or omissions brought to its attention so that they may be corrected in subsequent printings.

The publisher acknowledges Alamy, Bridgeman Images, Getty Images, and Shutterstock as its primary image suppliers for this title.